The Irvine Valley

Then and Now

By Hugh Maxwell

Many women of all ages, like those seen here, found employment at the brass bobbin winding within the lace factories in the Irvine Valley. In the days before mechanisation weaving women had also worked the handloom despite it being an industry dominated mostly by men; in Darvel in 1842 there were 61 female weavers besides 267 male weavers. Women were also responsible for winding the cotton or silk thread onto the pirns, clipping and then sewing, in addition to cleaning and cooking for the household. In later years with the introduction of the power loom women were again to play an important role and found employment in many areas of the industry. Just like the men they worked long hard shifts in hot and noisy conditions and their expertise in sewing and darning was much in demand. Women also worked the madras looms and designed the patterns although some did work in what was seen as more traditional clerical roles. This photograph shows the large wooden bobbins with the lace thread on the right being wound through the brass bobbin machine and onto the smaller brass bobbins.

Acknowledgements

The author would like to thank the many people of the Irvine Valley who were willing to contribute information towards this book and also friends and family for their generous support and assistance.

Further Reading

James Mair, *Pictorial History of Darvel*, Alloway Publishing, 1989.
James Mair, *Pictorial History of Newmilns*, Alloway Publishing, 1988.
James Mair, *Pictorial History of Galston*, Alloway Publishing, 1988.
Alex. G. McLeod, *The Book of Old Darvel*, Walker & Connell, *c.* early 1950s.
John Woodburn, *A History of Darvel*, Walker & Connell, 1967.
Newmilns and Greenholm Community Council, *Historical Aspects of Newmilns*, 1990.
John Macintosh, *Ayrshire Nights' Entertainments*, John Menzies, 1894.
John Strawhorn, *Ayrshire – The Story of a County*, Ayrshire Archaeological & Natural History Society, 1975.
Hugh Maxwell, *Old Darvel*, Stenlake Publishing Ltd, 2001.
Hugh Maxwell, *Old Newmilns*, Stenlake Publishing Ltd, 2001.
Hugh Maxwell, *Old Galston*, Stenlake Publishing Ltd, 2001.
Copies of the *Weekly Supplement and Advertiser* and the *Irvine Valley News* held within the Dick Institute, Kilmarnock.

Introduction

In prehistoric times the Irvine Valley was heavily forested but the natural topography of this valley provided a ready route for people travelling from the west coast through to the east. The strategic importance of this was recognised by the Romans who, between around 85 and 165 AD, had a large camp near the volcanic plug of Loudoun Hill, located at the head of the valley.

By the time of Robert the Bruce, who defeated an English army near Loudon Hill in 1307, small scattered dwellings existed throughout the valley but with the clearing of large areas of land for agriculture and fuel and the exploitation of the water for power this quickly changed. Numerous corn and meal mills were located along the banks of the River Irvine as it flowed down through the valley and this resulted in the creation of small close-knit hamlets. Soon the valley became an important trading route, carrying ever increasing amounts of goods and travellers and bringing considerable economic benefits to the local residents.

As a result of this, in 1490 Newmilns was officially created a Free Burgh of Barony in a charter granted by King James IV. This acknowledged the importance of the village which became the first inland burgh and the fifth burgh within Ayrshire. The inhabitants of the village were now empowered with the liberty to buy and sell all manner of goods and to hold regular fairs and markets. This was further reinforced in 1566 by Mary, Queen of Scots, when a charter was again granted empowering the burgh to hold its own court. In 1707 Newmilns became a Burgh of Regality, giving it greater powers of local jurisdiction.

Throughout the seventeenth century the people of the district were at the forefront of the struggle for religious freedom and suffered harsh persecution by government soldiers who were stationed at the keep in Newmilns. On one gruesome occasion they even played football on the Green in Newmilns with a martyr's head. When the National Covenant was drawn up in 1638 it held the signatures of countless men from the valley with 328 from Galston parish alone. The local religious troubles culminated in the Battle of Drumclog on 1 June 1679 when the Covenanters, mostly from the Irvine Valley district, defeated government troops under Claverhouse. The monuments and tombstones that stand within church graveyards commemorate these brave individuals.

Towards the close of the sixteenth century there had been an influx of Dutch and Huguenot immigrants to the valley and many brought with them their knowledge of spinning and weaving cloth. Their trade secrets quickly passed on to the local people and as a direct result the handloom weaving industry was born and increasing numbers of people began to find employment weaving the cloth. By 1791 forty hand looms were in operation in Galston while Newmilns had 266 weavers and Darvel a similar number weaving the cloth. Single-storey cottages were built along the main streets and as a result the populations of all three valley towns began to increase.
Following the Napoleonic Wars of the early nineteenth century there was a major slump in the trade of cotton and lean years of poverty, disease and semi-starvation followed. The principal industry in Darvel and Newmilns was now handloom weaving, whereas in Galston an equal number found employment at the loom or in farming. Many local landowners had begun to see the benefits of implementing agricultural improvements on their large estates and this was done extensively at Cessnock, Loudoun and Lanfine. As a result Galston became the centre of a thriving agricultural community.

By the mid 1800s the population of Darvel had risen dramatically to 1,360 with 267 male and 61 female weavers, the population of Newmilns had almost doubled to 1,988 with a staggering 460 male and 90 female weavers and in Galston the population had grown to 4,727. This rapid increase in population saw the valley towns expand quickly with many new streets being created and feus being granted for the building of houses on land that had previously lain bare.

In 1875 the introduction of the power loom at a mill in Darvel revolutionised the weaving industry and brought much prosperity and employment back to the Irvine Valley. The success of this venture by Alexander Morton saw many large factories being built in both Newmilns and Darvel. In Darvel by 1915 over 1,000 people found employment and there were as many as twenty factories in operation including associated trades. In Newmilns it had been a similar story with fourteen large mills being built in Greenholm and near the Green and by 1915 the population peaked at almost 5,000.

Galston was least affected by the decline in the handloom trade as coal mining that had been carried out on a small scale on the estate of Cessnock since the late eighteenth century was exploited commercially. This was aided by the expansion of the railway from Hurlford in 1848 and Galston became a centre for coal mining with as many as 1,100 men finding work in the fifteen local collieries. Two large lace mills had also been built in Galston and they also employed around 300 workers and a large woollen mill was also built.

With rising populations and chronic overcrowding it was in the years just after both world wars that many large council housing schemes were built in all three valley towns to provide much needed modern housing for the inhabitants. This continued into the 1950s and 1960s with many of the old dilapidated buildings that stood along main streets also being demolished to be replaced with modern housing.

In the 1930s the last of the pits in Galston closed and during the Second World War many of the valley mills closed down as workers went off to serve their country overseas. The factories were used mainly to store government equipment and supplies although some manufactured mosquito nets. After the war trade was slow and manufacturers were faced with changing fashions, increasing competition from overseas and the introduction of tariffs for exports. By the early 1970s almost half of the mills had either closed, gone out of business or had reduced significantly the number of shifts and workers they employed. The industry that had been booming prior to the outbreak of the war was now faced with decline.

Some manufacturers such as Stiebel & Co. in Darvel began to manufacture and market products from new synthetic materials such as Terylene. When this proved to be a successful venture many of the remaining factories began to change over to Terylene although they still continued to work the lace, manufacturing a mixture of textile goods. However, the decline continued and factory after factory went out of business. In the Irvine Valley today there remains only a handful of textile companies left. Many of the old factory sites have since been redeveloped for housing and the towns have attracted incomers and developed as dormitory communities. The area is rich in history and scenery and despite many changes the towns have retained much of their original character and charm.

Priestland is a small hamlet located just east of Darvel, adjacent the main road as it travels towards Loudoun Hill and onwards to Strathaven. This view from the 1940s shows the bus that travelled from Hamilton via Strathaven through the valley to Kilmarnock and then to its final destination down the coast at Ayr. Priestland was originally part of Galston Parish and was a separate little community with its own grocers' shops such as Gracie's and Smith's. It also had its own corn mill on the banks of the River Irvine. A number of council houses were later built, in keeping with the character of the hamlet, just out of view on the right at Loudoun Avenue; a small number of private houses have also been added at Crofthead. Today little has changed in this scene with the houses looking almost exactly as they have done for the last 100 years.

Looking westwards along the main road into Darvel in October 1920 with the corn mill visible on the right. The mill was served by a lade that ran from the Mill Dam which was located between the east end of Darvel and where the road turns sharply towards the hamlet of Priestland. The lade itself ran along the north side of the road and often became blocked with stones, silt and other debris. Frequently children would play in the lade and during the summer months could be found guddling for brown trout under the stones. The mill was badly damaged by fire in the 1920s and later demolished when the lade was also filled in. Just out of view on the left was the large lace mill of Morton, Aird and Co., established in 1900, while in the distance is the Glen Brig carrying the main road over the Glen Water. It was at an old clipping mill next to the Brig that Alexander Morton introduced the power loom in 1875, transforming the weaving industry within the Irvine Valley. Today much has changed in this view with large private housing schemes being built adjacent the main road on George Young Drive and Green Bank Road. Only a small stone wall now marks the site of the corn mill, and the lace factories at the Glen Brig have also been replaced by private housing.

Page 5

Page 6

Page 8

Page 9

Looking eastwards along East Main Street in October 1920, towards Glen Brig and the area that became known as the Townhead of Darvel. With its mile-long main street, the village was commonly known as the 'Lang Toon'. Lining both sides of the street are many of the original single-storey thatched handloom weavers' cottages, dating back to the late eighteenth and nineteenth centuries. The handloom weavers were an independent, self-reliant and hard working class who spent many long hours, day and night, at their wooden looms plying the shuttle to earn an honest living. They enjoyed some prosperous days but times were often hard with much unemployment. To avoid actual starvation for themselves and their families the weavers often resorted to what was known locally as 'cadging', the selling of all manner of cloths and apparel, needles, thread and even home baking to those who lived in the countryside. These would be bartered in return for cash or for farm produce. Many of the original single-storey handloom weavers' cottages in this view have now been replaced by modern housing but some still remain.

Kirkland Road branched off East Main Street in the Townhead and this is the view looking northwards. On the right is the large hedge surrounding the grounds of Kirkland Park and house, home of Alexander Morton, lace manufacturer. The street took its name from the kirklands of Darvel that once covered a large area and further up the road there also once existed the Clen Chapel. Just out of view near the top of the street was the railway bridge and banking that carried the railway line from Strathaven. Beyond this were the playing fields used by the junior football teams of the day. In later years a large number of council houses were built at the top of Kirkland Road and private housing was also built on the grounds of Kirkland Park, the house now an unsightly ruin.

A view from the late 1940s of the housing scheme at the top of Kirkland Road, taken from the area known locally as the Laggan. Work on these houses started in the late 1930s. The Glen Water, one of the tributaries of the River Irvine, is visible on the left and in the foreground is the winding street of Glen Crescent followed by Paterson Terrace leading down onto Kirkland Road with the houses on Hutchinson Drive still being constructed. On the left the railway line from Strathaven can be seen crossing Kirkland Road and heading towards the station on Jamieson Road whilst in the foreground are the market gardens and greenhouses that once existed in the fields behind some of the houses. Little has changed in this scene today and this large scheme, which was built on the edge of the countryside in the Glen, has become a desirable place to live within the town.

A procession marking the occasion of the funeral of King Edward VII on 20 May 1910, travelling west along East Main Street. The people of Darvel were well versed in processions through the streets for the annual parade or 'prawd' as it was known locally. Originally held on New Year's Day and headed by the village band, the men would turn out in their Sunday best and wearing sashes and would then march up and down the Main Street in slow procession. They would be carrying swords, pikes and staves and would also walk past the Dagon Stone at the Cross as a mark of superstitious respect. A Wee Race for boys was also held on Main Street in the afternoon. In later years during the summer the Gala Parade would travel along Main Street headed by the lace queen. Every factory or local group would enter a float based on a theme, with prizes being awarded to the winners at Morton Park. In the background of this photograph is the grocer's shop run by Robert Rogerson that later became Gemmell's and is still run as a small grocer's today. The scene has since changed considerably: the thatched building on the left has been replaced with a modern Co-op store while almost all of the thatched houses to the right of the grocer's shop have been replaced with council housing.

Page 10

Premier
Darvel Convenience Store
Page 11

TopUp here!
NEWSAGENTS
POST OFFICE
PayPoint
Page 13

30
30
Page 14

Looking westwards along Main Street towards the Cross and Hastings Square from the junction of Jamieson Road, 1950. On the left are the hardware and bakery shops belonging to the Co-operative, followed by the Medical Hall and dispensing chemists. Next, at the corner of Ranoldcoup Road, are the central premises of the Darvel Industrial Co-operative Society Ltd., which were built on the site of the Black Bull Inn. Downstairs was the grocery department whilst upstairs was a large hall with a wooden floor that was frequently used for dancing. It was here at the Cross, at the head of Ranoldcoup Road, that the iron toll gates once stood on the turnpike road, raising tolls from travelling coaches and horse riders until 1889 when they ceased to be used. This was also the place where the handloom weavers often gathered to discuss the serious political and religious subjects of the day. The toll gates have since been restored and are now situated further down Ranoldcoup Road on display in a small memorial garden overlooking the junction of Collins Avenue. The co-operative shops on the left have now been mostly demolished after being derelict for many years while across the street some of the older buildings near the junction of Cross Street have been replaced with modern housing.

Looking along East Donnington Street from the junction of Jamieson Road, May 1928. East and West Donnington streets date from the late nineteenth century when it was decided a long street mirroring Main Street was needed. This was a quiet residential area away from the bustling main road and many detached and semi-detached villas and sandstone flats were quickly built. In this view a motorbike and sidecar can be seen stopped in the middle of the street near the police station, the building with the chimney stack third on the right. Darvel once had its own resident constable from the Ayrshire Constabulary and if someone was apprehended for committing a crime they faced being arrested and locked up in the small cell at the back of the station before being charged for their misdemeanours. The police station closed in 1973 and was moved to West Main Street but this has now also closed.

This is the opposite view looking along West Donnington Street from near the junction of Cross Street, May 1928. Visible on the right are the cherry trees in the grounds of the Original Secession Church and manse that was built in 1883, while at the end of the street are the factory buildings of Alexander Jamieson and Co., the largest lace manufacturer within the town. Established in 1887, over 350 men and women were employed making fine lace and madras goods such as curtains and bed covers for both domestic and foreign markets. The factory buildings have since been replaced by modern private housing in the form of Lace Mill Wynd.

A 1920s view looking east along the tracks towards the iron footbridge that connects the two platforms at Darvel railway station. The railway reached Darvel in June 1896, having been extended east from Newmilns, and was operated by the Glasgow and South Western Railway Company. The terminus and goods yard were located near the top of Jamieson Road and in May 1905 the line was extended further east to Strathaven. The station was always a hive of activity as trains brought workers to and from the thriving lace mills and also enabled raw materials and finished goods to be despatched easily and quickly. Just out of view on the right were the goods yard, sidings and turntable. Following decreasing passenger numbers and goods transport, and also sweeping government cuts, the line was closed in 1964. The brick chimney and buildings on the left belong to the lace factory of John Aird & Co. which was established in 1896 and became known locally as 'Joke Aird's'. Today a large private housing scheme named Station Gate occupies the site of the station, and no evidence of it remains. The factory has also been replaced with private housing.

Page 15

Page 16

Page 18

Page 19

The Public School was opened by the Loudoun School Board on 5 January 1904. Located at the top of Jamieson Road, it cost £10,000 and was built from red Ballochmyle sandstone. It was able to provide education for up to 350 scholars. In this view a little girl can be seen standing on Campbell Street while in the background the west entrance for the boys is visible with the girl's entrance on the east side of the school. Many residents of the town, including the author, have fond memories of playing games in the large playground during break times. In April 2011 work was undertaken by the local council to refurbish and extend the school at a cost of £5 million. A large extension now houses a nursery unit and this is connected onto the school with a link corridor. Work finished in the summer of 2012 and now the nursery school has relocated from the old buildings in Ranoldcoup Road to the new school extension which is now stands to the right of this view.

Hastings Square in May 1928, with three buses and their drivers waiting to transport the large numbers of factory workers who would soon be 'clocking off' from their shifts at the lace factories. The war memorial was erected in the early 1920s to honour the fallen from the Great War and was later inscribed with the names of those who perished in the Second World War. Visible across Main Street is the large red sandstone frontage of the Town Hall, built in 1905 at a cost of £15,000, and on its left is the grocers shop run by M. and C. Scade. Hastings Square and the Town Hall still remain at the centre of the town's activities. Since 2001 the hall has also now become the venue each spring for the popular Darvel Music Festival which attracts quality musicians, performers and visitors from locally and much further afield. The square now houses the Dagon Stone and the Alexander Fleming Memorial bust and garden.

Looking north up the steep Burn Road in October 1920 with the photographer standing just beyond the railway bridge. On the right can be seen the red sandstone cottages dating from around 1900, followed by the junction of Campbell Street, while further up the hill are the trees in the grounds of 'The Braes'. This was the mansion home of Alexander Jamieson, provost of the town and a successful lace manufacturer who built the largest factory in town on Burn Road in 1887. This manufactured quality lace and madras products for the home and export markets such as curtains, table covers and tapestries. Burn Road takes its name from the Matthew Burn which flows down off the surrounding fields into the village alongside the left side of the road in this view. This road was also part of a popular countryside walk known locally as the '5-mile' which ends near the new cemetery. Private housing has since been built along both sides of Burn Road.

Townhead, looking east into Isles Street with Darvel Road disappearing up the 'Cut' around 1905. On the right is the lace factory that belonged to Henderson, Morton and Inglis which was built in 1893. In 1954 this scene looked considerably different when the town coup at Isle Public Park was washed down into the Norrel Burn after continuous heavy rain for several days. The burn normally flows under the streets and houses before emptying into the River Irvine at the Green; however, it had become blocked with many years of rubbish and totally flooded this area of the town. A wall of mud and rubbish flowed down Darvel Road engulfing everything in its path and considerable damage was done to local businesses and homes. Campbell Street, Union Street, Main Street and Burn Road were covered in thick layers of mud and a double-decker bus trying to negotiate the Cut was even shoved into a hedge by the force of the deluge. The lace mill closed down in the 1980s and after a large fire destroyed most of the interior of the building it was demolished and a private housing scheme named Weavers Place was built. The houses visible on Isles Street were subsequently demolished in the late 1950s and early 1960s when a large number of modern council houses were constructed here and along Campbell Street.

Page 20

Page 21

THE CROWN HOTEL
GOOD FOOD SERVED
ALL DAY
ACCOMMODATION
CAR PARK
Page 23

BUS STOP
Page 24

An early 1900s view of Townhead, looking west along Main Street from Isles Street, with the steeple of the Loudoun Parish Church visible in the distance. On the right the gable sign advertises the Townhead Athletic Bar (also known as the Angel Inn). The junction seen here is with Back Street, now know as King Street, which led to the gas works and the Free church. This popular public house was the last stop for both players and supporters as they travelled up the Cut to Hillhead Park near Alstonpapple for the football matches, hence its name. Across Main Street on the left is the single-storey thatched cottage that was Auld's Dairy, later to become Gilmour's, followed by the frontage of the Crown Hotel. Prior to the outbreak of the Second World War many of the buildings on the right of the Main Street were demolished by the burgh council to help widen the road for the increasing amount of traffic. Today, the Crown Hotel remains popular with locals and the single-storey thatched cottage on the left of this view still stands.

Looking west along Main Street in 1956 towards the Cross with the grounds of Lady Flora's Institute visible on the right followed by the red sandstone Morton Hall which was opened in 1896. Across Main Street is the small grocer's and spirits shop owned by James Morris, followed by the sandstone pend which led through to the workshops of Joseph Hood, inventor, engineer and loom builder, where 24 people were employed manufacturing sewing frames and jacquard weaving machines. Further on the gable jutting out belongs to what was once was the Newmilns Temperance Hotel and then there are the railings surrounding the parish church with the Covenanter's Monument visible in the corner of the graveyard next to the East Strand. The row of two-storey buildings leading up to the church was demolished in the 1960s and replaced with council houses.

This view from the Institute Brig over the River Irvine, taken around 1904, shows Greenside and Loudoun Parish Church. The house on the far left dates from 1781 and was once the parish school and schoolhouse until it closed in 1872 whereby it became a private dwelling. It was then replaced with the church hall in 1934. A plaque on the wall commemorates the school which had up to 90 scholars. The last schoolmaster was John Lyon Campbell. Across the East Strand is the 'Beadle's House' followed by the wall enclosing the church graveyard where many interesting tombstones are located, most notably the 1823 memorial to the Covenanting martyr, John Nisbet. He had fought at the Battle of Drumclog and was later captured by soldiers after being wounded six times. He was taken to Edinburgh and executed on the Grassmarket. The parish church was erected in 1844 on the site of an older building dating from 1738. It opened for public worship on Sunday, 14 September 1845 and was renovated 50 years later when an organ was purchased by the congregation. It was most likely designed by James Ingram.

Dating from the early nineteenth century, Greenside House was once one of the oldest houses in Newmilns. It looked onto the common ground bordered by the River Irvine known as 'The Green.' This was also where the Annual Trades Races took place and it was the venue for travelling shows, meetings and fairs. Held every July, the Trades Races began in 1743 and were organised by the Incorporated Trades of Newmilns. Events included the 100-metre sprint, the skipping rope race and the greasy pole, with prizes of cash or goods drawn from local shops. The races ceased around 1920 due to lack of interest. In 1895 the 26-arched railway viaduct was constructed, cutting the 'The Green' in half when the railway was extended to Darvel. Greenside House and other old houses and tenements were demolished and replaced with council housing in the 1960s but 'The Green' remains a pleasant area next to the river.

Page 25

Page 26

Page 28

Page 29

Newmilns Public School, 1914. The school was built in 1894 by the Loudoun School Board and overlooked the town and the wooded policies of Lanfine, just off High Street. It was designed by the architect John Macintosh who lived at the nearby Strath Mill on the banks of the River Irvine. On its opening day 381 boys and 106 girls attended under the tutelage of Headmaster Archibald Hood. The school was known locally as 'Hood's School' and provided primary and higher education until Monday, 1February 1960, when it was badly damaged by fire. Its elevated position ultimately led to its destruction as the gusting breeze fanned the flames through its wooden timbers leaving just a stone shell and only three usable classrooms. Education continued in temporary wooden huts until 1964 when a new primary school was opened near Gilfoot. In 1971 Loudoun Academy was opened to cater for all the secondary pupils from the valley towns. Today the elevated site has been developed into a challenging downhill bike park and a dry ski slope.

A 1956 view looking east along Main Street towards the Cross. Further along the street is the distinctive three-storey Loudoun Arms, standing at the corner of Castle Street, just after the building with the hanging sign. This dates from the eighteenth century and was once frequented by Robert Burns. The keep in Castle Street is the oldest building in town, dating from the sixteenth century and is an old fortified tower house built by the Campbells of Loudoun. The two-storey white building on the right of the photograph is the auld cooncil house which dates from 1739.

Main Street looking into Kilnholm Street around 1906 with the drinking fountain visible on the left at the Bridgend Corner which was often referred to as the 'Fuddle' by locals. The fountain was gifted to the village by Provost Joseph Hood and was erected in 1890 to mark the installation of the gravitational water supply which ran from the reservoir near Loudoun Hill. Visible on the left at the 'Brigend Corner' is Mr Rawlinson's Hotel which later became the Brigend Inn, while across the main road is the distinctive red sandstone frontage of the central premises of the Co-operative Society. Built on the corner of High Street and Main Street, it was constructed in 1900 and housed the various departments of the Co-operative on the two floors as well as a large social hall. In 1908 a large fire completely gutted the building, resulting in around £8,000 worth of damage but it was immediately repaired and today it now houses modern flats. The fountain was eventually removed in the late 1940s when it became a hazard to motorists and the Bridgend Inn has also since closed.

Looking west along Brown Street in 1923 from near the Greenholm Bridge that spans the River Irvine. On the right is the Railway Hotel which was formerly known as the Lamlash Inn and is now called the Riverside Inn (it is still often referred to as the 'Railway' by locals). Further down, across the junction of Nelson Street or the 'Water Wynd' as it is known locally, is the sandstone building housing the post office which was erected in 1908. Many of the cottages that lined Brown Street dated from the middle of the nineteenth century and housed the handloom weavers and their families as the trade flourished at this time. Brown Street was once one of the busiest thoroughfares in the town as it led directly to the railway station and goods yard and also the many large lace mills but with the closure of the line and the mills in the early 1960s much of the hustle and bustle has disappeared. Otherwise little has changed today: the post office is still in the same building and the Riverside Inn remains popular with locals.

Page 30

Page 31

Page 33

Page 34

Looking east along the tracks at Newmilns railway station in August 1958. Visible in the distance is the Tileworks Brig leading up to Mount Pleasant Farm surrounded by trees. The railway reached Newmilns in 1850 with the original small station being replaced with a much larger station and goods yard in 1890. Located on Brown Street, it was one of the busiest places in the town as workers arrived in the mornings or travelled to Darvel or Galston to start their shifts in the lace mills. The line on the left was frequently the up line whilst that on the right was often the down line. The railway closed during the early 1960s and the site was later occupied by the extensive buildings of the Vesuvius Crucible Company, sadly now closed. The factory made furnace and foundry products for the steel industry.

In this photograph from 1907 the River Irvine flows past the houses on Kilnholm Street, while on the right is the ornamental bandstand in Greenholm. The bandstand was erected at the turn of the century and on balmy summer evenings large crowds would frequently gather to listen to musical performances of the 'Burgh Baun' as they conducted open air rehearsals and performances. The bandstand eventually fell into disrepair and what had once been a beautiful ornate iron and glass structure was finally torn down and removed by the council prior to the outbreak of the Second World War. Only the metal railings and brick wall now remain. Following the devastating 'Lammas Floods' in August 1920, when a large section of Kilnholm Street was swept away with the flow of the water, the road was rebuilt and the bankings were also strengthened with a proper wall as can be seen in this photograph. Kilnholm Street took its name from the lime workings and limekilns that were once located in the fields behind the houses. Little has changed in this scene today with only more private housing having been built up the Borebrae. On the far left are the large three-storey sandstone flats which were known locally as the 'Glesca Buildings' due to their resemblance to the Glasgow tenements. Due to their weight and proximity to the river, they began to subside and were demolished in 1986.

Looking east along Riverbank Street from Shields Road, *c.* 1909. In the background are the factory buildings of Hood Morton & Co. Ltd., lace and madras manufacturers established in 1867. The factory was on Nelson Street in Greenholm. It was the first powerloom mill in Newmilns and was located on the banks of the River Irvine to harness the water for the steam engine that powered the machines. Originally it produced what was called wincey goods, a mixture of cotton and wool and it was known locally as the Wincey Mill. The partners in this enterprise were local men Joseph Hood, a loom builder, and Hugh Morton, a weaving agent. The factory later expanded to manufacture lace, madras, chenille and also tapestry goods. The towering brick chimney that is visible above the rooftops belongs to another textile manufacturer, Haddow, Aird and Crerar Ltd, established in 1881, and on the corner of the street can be seen one of the many dressmakers' shops that once existed within the village.

Looking northwards in 1956 across the railway tracks and the River Irvine, towards the large council scheme of Gilfoot and the playing field on the north side of the main road. To alleviate the chronic overcrowding 127 houses were built in the village between 1936 and 1939. Many families chose to live in Newmilns at this time as work could readily be found in the numerous lace mills. On the right can be seen the council scheme at Masons Holm which was built on the south side of the main road following the end of the Second World War.

Page 35

Page 36

Page 38

Page 39

This is the view looking south towards Galston in the late 1950s where a motor car can be seen exiting the junction for the main Edinburgh road that led up the valley to Newmilns and Darvel. The photographer is standing on the A719 main road that ran from Ayr through Galston and onwards to Moscow and Waterside. This route was always busy during the summer months as day trippers travelled down from Glasgow to the coast and, as the traffic also increased on the road from Edinburgh down the valley, the town would frequently become congested at the Four Corners. As a result, in the late 1970s the Galston by-pass was constructed to divert much of the through traffic away from the town. A large roundabout replaced the junction in this photograph and further west a new bridge carries the main road over the River Irvine.

A view from around 1923 looking north from Wallace Street towards the Four Corners and into Polwarth Street, with the hump of the Muckle Brig visible beyond. On the left at the bottom of the street is the distinctive frontage of the Co-operative Society building built in 1889. Across the street is the thatched roof of the Railway Inn; following a fire in 1974 it was officially renamed what locals had always affectionately known it – the Wee Train. Further down the street at number 12 is the ironmongers of T. Black & Sons, established in 1851. In the *Ayrshire Directory* of 1837 Galston was thus described: 'The principal employment of the labouring class is weaving, there is manufactory for muslins, another for linens and three for bonnets. The stream of the river, which is crossed by a stone bridge of three arches, gives motion to 2 corn-mills, another for preparing flax, and one for making paper; besides these various means of employment, another occupation is found in raising coals, of which a considerable quantity is obtained from estates of the Duke of Portland, who is superior of the parish.'

Opened in 1912 in Wallace Street, the picture house quickly became one of the busiest entertainment venues in town. The original façade of the building with its impressive flagpole (opposite) were later replaced with the more modern, albeit drab looking, grey concrete and roughcast exterior visible in this photograph. With the advent of television the crowds slowly dwindled and it closed in 1968. By the time of this photograph from June 1985 the building housed the Valley Veterinary Centre. It has since been demolished and private flats have been built on the site.

The Picture House, Galston

Barr Castle, 1900. This fortified tower house dates from the fifteenth century when it was occupied by the Lockharts of Barr and is Galston's oldest building. Frequent shouts of 'gemme ba' were once heard echoing around its north wall as the game of handball was played. Large crowds that had surrounded the 'Baur Ailley' would erupt with cheers and applause at the contests which decided the new winners of the Galston Handball Challenge Cup. The origins of the game here are vague, but it reached its peak in the years leading up to the First World War. At that time the Champion of the Alley was held in high renown and local legends such as wily Jock Adam, the invincible Black Tott and the ever reliable Red Wullie once graced the 'Baur Ailley' with their athleticism, skill and deft touches. Today the game is but a fond memory for some of the town's older inhabitants and the castle is now owned by the Galston Masonic Fraternity Lodge St. Peter 331 which has restored it and also created a small museum on the top floor. In the background is the distinctive steeple of the Trinity Free Church which was built in 1887/88 in the Glebe Knowes field, while in the foreground on Wallace Street is the Erskine Free Church, built in 1859. The Trinity Free Church was demolished in 1963 and the Erskine Free Church was later converted into luxury private flats. The two single-storey cottages dating from the early nineteenth century were also later demolished and replaced with a modern bungalow.

Pages 40 & 41

Page 42

Page 44

Page 45

A 1956 view from Henrietta Street, looking across the Four Corners into Bridge Street. On the right is the junction of Polwarth Street while on the left is the junction of Wallace Street. This is the busiest area of the town and suffered most from traffic congestion when motor vehicles became commonplace. As a result metal railings were erected to protect pedestrians as motorists negotiated the sharp corners and a Zebra Crossing, visible in this scene, was erected in Bridge Street. In the distance can be seen the Portland Arms Hotel at the 'Portland Corner' while the small seated area in the right foreground was previously the site of the Commercial Inn.

Looking east into Bridge Street in the early 1900s from near the junction of Cross Street with the Four Corners and Henrietta Street visible in the distance. On the left is the corner of the Portland Arms Hotel and the children are standing in the area that became known locally as the Portland Corner. On the right are the ornamental railings surrounding the British Linen Bank and further down the street were the premises and shop of William McDonald and Sons, printers and stationers, who for many years published the local newspaper the Weekly Supplement and Advertiser which reported on all the news from Hurlford, Galston, Newmilns and Darvel. Just below the gable advertising for the Black Bull Hotel can be seen the bridge over the Burn Anne which flows under and gives the street its name.

A very early twentieth century view of the bottom of Brewland Street with the parish church, dating from 1808/09, dominating the scene. The street can be seen sweeping sharply to the right past the handloom weavers' thatched cottages into Bridge Street. From the twelfth century Galston became an important ecclesiastical centre and Brewland Street may have taken its name from the local monks or friars who once brewed ale, beers and whisky in this area. This scene has changed considerably today with the large central premises of the Co-operative Society building now standing on the right and dating from around 1901. The old cottages in the centre of the scene have also been demolished to widen the main road and the parish church now has a chancel which was added to the rear. During the late 1950s and throughout the 1960s many modern houses and flats were built at the bottom of the street but in recent years the council flats have since been demolished.

PARISH CHURCH GALSTON
RELIABLE SERIES 2402

Looking northwest along Duke Street from near the railway station with the premises of J. and W. Wilson contractors visible at the corner of Duke Street and Station Road. Their horses and carts were a common sight throughout the valley and in addition to carrying goods and coal they were also undertakers. The firm did not change to mechanised transport and ceased trading shortly after the Second World War, whereby the premises were converted into private housing. On the left are two of the original railway workers' cottages that were also later converted into private dwellings when the railway closed.

Pages 46 & 47

Page 48

Page 50

Page 51

Two young ladies waiting on the platform at Galston railway station in the 1950s. The station was opened in 1848 by the Glasgow and South Western Railway Company who had extended the line east from Hurlford to help transport the coal that was mined locally. The photographer is standing on the bridge at Station Road which spans the lines and is looking east with the waiting room on the right and the station offices and goods yard on the left. Just behind the goods yard are the newly built council houses on Blair Crescent. The line and station were closed in August 1966 and a large telephone exchange building now occupies the site. A private housing scheme named Belvedere View was built along the course of the line and on part of Duke Street.

A view from c. 1903 taken on the Sorn Road, looking northwards into Cessnock Road with the distinctive row of Burnhouse Cottages in the foreground. These were once lived in by many of the workers and their families of the nearby Cessnock Castle and estate. On the right Clockston Road can also be seen heading into the countryside towards Newmilns and the Gallowlaw Cairn. On the left is the road that leads down to the Bridge House and along past the cemetery on Cemetery Road. This scene has changed considerably. The cottages were demolished after the Second World War and many private villas built adjacent the Cessnock and Clockston roads. The open fields that lay behind the cottages are now occupied by the large private housing scheme of Sorn Place and Burnawn Place.

Looking west along Bentinck Street, once known as Bentinck Terrace, around 1910. The distinctive red brick St Sophia's RC Church and school are on the left. Built in the years 1885/56, the church was freely modelled on the Hagia Sophia in Istanbul, Turkey, and was funded by the 3rd Marquis of Bute. With its large circular tower rising from the centre and its slightly elevated position overlooking the town, the church is one of the most distinctive buildings in the area. The photographer was standing at the junction of Blair Street and in the distance can be seen the Glebe Public School on the Glebe Road and also the Erskine Free Church. Little has changed in this view although the church school has since been closed and converted into a private dwelling and council houses were later built at the corner of Bentinck and Blair Street.

Looking north along Orchard Street towards the junction with Titchfield Street and into Gas Lane in the early 1900s. The street took its name from the old parish church orchards that once existed in this area and many of the houses in this view date from the early to mid nineteenth century. In the *Ayrshire Directory* of 1837 some of the tradesmen who lived in the street were: 'Agent to Manufacturers – John Goldie and Robert Mair; Boot and Shoe Maker – Michael McDonald; Grocer and Spirit Dealer – Marths Wallace; Joiner – Robert Parlane; Manufacturer – Robert Mair (Linen); Slater – Cunningham Hutchinson; Stone Mason – Robert Wallace; and Tailor – George Marsh.' In later years some of the old tenements on the left were knocked down and Milton Road was created, while many of the old cottages that were once occupied by the miners and handloom weavers have since been modernised.

Page 52

Page 53

Page 55

Page 56

The Old Men's Cabin, surrounded by its colourful flower beds and flagged paths on Milton Road in 1956. This was where retired men of the town could go to chat and play cards. In the background are Portland Park and the newly built council houses on Ladyton Drive and Western Road. These had been built to provide modern homes for many of the families who had once lived in the old Taurry and Gauchalland rows. Following the closure of many of the local pits these rows of slum-like houses were demolished by the burgh council and an extensive house building scheme was undertaken. Little has changed in this view today with only an extension being added to the rear of the cabin itself and the disappearance of the flower beds and flagstones to be replaced with grass.

Located just to the north of Galston near Loudoun Castle, Loudounkirk was a small row of cottages that stood at the side of a quiet country road in a sheltered corner of the Irvine Valley. The cottages were named after the nearby Loudoun Kirk, the burial chamber for the Campbells of Loudoun, which is just out of view at the end of the road in this photograph from 1923 looking west. South facing, in the summer the whitewashed walls of the cottages were always covered in sweet scented climbing plants such as woodbine, honeysuckle and roses. Less than a hundred people lived here with many of them finding employment in the extensive Loudoun Castle and estate. The cottages dated from the 1850s and later housed some of the miners and their families who worked in the nearby Loudoun collieries. This scene was still recognisable up until the 1930s when many of the families began to move out and by the end of the Second World War the cottages had been abandoned and were later demolished.